UNDERSTANDING
THE LAST DAYS
OF HIS-STORY
MOVING TOWARD ETERNITY

MARY ANN MATSON

outskirtspress

DENVER, COLORADO

Outskirts Press, Inc.
http://www.outskirtspress.com

ISBN: 978-1-4787-5296-7

Outskirts Press and the "OP" logo are trademarks belonging to Outskirts Press, Inc.

PRINTED IN THE UNITED STATES OF AMERICA

Acknowledgments

I acknowledge my Lord and Savior Jesus Christ as not only the author and finisher of my faith but in the completion of this book as well. Hebrews 12:1 encourages us to run with patience the race that is set before us by laying aside every weight and sin which slows us down. The race we are in is a lifelong test of faith in this world to win the prize. The prize being the incorruptible crown of gaining eternal salvation, the precious goal of the Christian life.

As a 40 year runner of marathons and 10K races, my ability and my desire to press on to finish the race and receive the prize of victory and achievement is a joyful experience in completing the work to which God has called me to do.

Table of Contents

Preface

We live in a day of perilous times. Every day the news is filled with disturbing events from the Middle East and around the world. No amount of effort can stop the clock of history. No mortal, no matter how influential, wealthy, or well known, can break the march of time. Each day that passes brings us closer to the dramatic events predicted in the Bible. We can prepare for the inevitable. We can put time to good use, but we cannot stop it; not for a moment. That can be an unsettling thought.

When we read about prophecy, we come across foreign terms like "the rapture," "the great tribulation," "the return of Jesus Christ," "the great white throne judgment," and "the lake of fire." Why is Bible prophecy important? Considered by itself, Messianic prophecy alone is proof that the Bible is the Word of God and no other. How else could the 39 separate books in the Old Testament, written by more than 30 different authors beginning in 3500 B.C., all describe in detail the life and death of One Person, narrated in four separate biographies hundreds of years in the future?

Blaise Pascal, French physicist, inventor, mathematician, Christian philosopher (17th century) once stated, "I have examined whether this God has not left some sign of Himself. I see many contradictory religions, and consequently all false save one. Each wants to be believed on its own authority, and threatens unbelievers. I do not therefore believe them. Every one can say this; every one can call himself a prophet. But I see that Christian religion wherein prophecies are fulfilled; and that is what every one cannot do." However, there are some stumbling blocks with what people are willing to believe and not to believe about prophecy. People with a conviction are hard to change since there are varying degrees of reality to them. Tell them you disagree and they turn away. Show them facts and figures and they question your sources. Appeal to logic and they fail to see your point of view.

Perhaps many of disagreements that divide us are rooted in our natural instincts for survival. To protect our beliefs and emotional attachments, we push threatening ideas away, and pull friendly information closer. This begins to happen subconsciously even before we are aware of what is happening. Self-protective reactions mobilize thoughts and emotions to protect our beliefs as if our lives depended on it. Therefore, leading with the facts on Biblical truths is probably not the best way to convince people to change their mind because invariably they won't. It is much wiser to begin by connecting with the values of the persons involved.

Since this book cannot connect with every reader's belief system, it is only recommended that they give facts of Biblical principles a fighting chance---as if our lives depended on it. In fact, someday we will have to give an account at the judgment seat of Christ. Jesus himself said about the Old Testament predictions, "This is what I told you while I was still with you: Everything must be fulfilled that is written about me in the Law of Moses; the Prophets, and the Psalms" (Luke 24:44). The book you are about to read has a start and a finish; exactly as the last days of history.

Setting the Stage

**What man can live and not see death, or save
himself from the power of the grave?
Psalm 89:48**

What a crushing and desperate thought! Life, however, is most dis-
appointing, most despairing, when it is lived as though this world is
all we have. Thankfully, this is not the only world. Christ connects us
to the eternal world and provides for us an eternally redeemed world
within each of us. Eternity is primary for all of us. We need to choose
where we will spend it. Heaven must become our first and ultimate
point of reference. We are built for it, redeemed for it, and on our way
to it. This present world is a place created by God for His glory, His
gain, and our enjoyment, but it is a place corrupted by the fall and
crowded with a fallen race. Our problem is that we don't spend enough
time trying to figure out our destiny in order to overcome the obstacles
of our present reality. However, we are called to view the reality of this
present world clearly, embrace the world beyond, and live a spirit-filled
life. While most all of us would like to embrace the reality of the world
to come, for many it seems neither real nor relevant.

The world's view of eternity tempers our tolerance and political correctness, and we relinquish ground unnecessarily to move forward searching for the truth that will set us free. After all, the world around us is a dangerous and destructive environment that, when left to itself, creates tension and trouble. For instance, we are often pressed with the reality of eternity only when a loved one dies. Or when we grow old and begin to realize that most of our lives have passed, and we note with regret the little we have done for eternity; the little we will take with us there and the short time left to do anything of significance for heaven's sake. This present world makes sense only when we live here in light of these other worlds. As Paul said "If in this life *only* we have hope in Christ, we are of all men most miserable" (1 Corinthians15:19). The tension of this world represents a phenomenal pressure. Yet we must constantly encourage each other with the truth that He has called us to be triumphant – not timid.

What we must remember, however, is that when Christ warned of the trouble we would face in this world, He wrapped the warning in the fact that we can find peace in Him and confidence in the fact that He has overcome the world. He said, "I have told you these things, so that in me you may have peace. In this world you will have trouble. But take heart! I have overcome the world" (John 16:33).

However, 1 John 5:19 states-"And we know that we are of God, and the whole world lieth in wickedness". What does that mean? We will never adequately understand the New Testament unless we recognize its underlying conviction that Satan is the *god* of this world and holds power over and controls much of the activity of this present age. His rule is usurped, however, temporary and not absolute. He continues only by the permissive will of God until the end of history as you will see throughout the reading of this book.

Scripture does not teach that God is now in direct control of the ungodly world, involving sinful people, evil, cruelty, injustice, and wickedness. In no way does God desire or cause all the suffering in the world, nor is everything that happens considered to be the perfect will of God. However, who do people blame when calamity comes upon people and the earth? God, of course. The Bible indicates that at the present time, the world is not under God's dominion, but is in rebellion against His rule and is enslaved to Satan. However, there is a sense in which God is in control of the ungodly world. God is sovereign and thus all things happen under His permissive will and oversight or at times through His direct involvement according to His purpose. Therefore, those who do not submit themselves to Jesus Christ remain under Satan's sway. Satan blinds their eyes to the truth and glory of the gospel in order that they might not be saved. Yet, this self-limitation is only temporary, for at the time determined by His wisdom, He will destroy all evil and Satan.

A good illustration of how Satan operates is in the book of Job that wrestles with the age-old question, why do the righteous suffer? Satan received permission to test the genuiness of the faith of Job. God's grace triumphed over Job's suffering because Job remained steadfast and immovable even under severe persecution. We do not always understand why God's dealings at times may seem dark and cruel but as in Job's case God is seen to be full of compassion and mercy at the end of Job's suffering.

Ultimately, in His time, this present world will come to a reckoning as the world to come overtakes this fallen, fading world. Therefore, it should come as no surprise that the last days of history should be upon us if not already. The ultimate goal is to prepare believers and non-believers for not only the last days but to forewarn them of the course of events to follow. The Bible describes in clear and unmistakable language how we should react to the word of God in all its different forms. In fact, Jesus himself states, "There is a judge for the one who rejects me and does not accept my words; that very word which I spoke will condemn him at the last day"(John 12:48). May you have ears to hear what the Spirit of God is saying to you as you read this book.

1

Last Days of Preparation

GODLESSNESS IN THE LAST DAYS

"But mark this: There will be terrible times in the last days. People will be lovers of themselves, lovers of money, boastful, proud, abusive, disobedient to their parents, ungrateful, unholy, without love, unforgiving, slanderous, without self-control, brutal, not lovers of the good, treacherous, rash, conceited, lovers of pleasure rather than lovers of God – having a form of godliness but denying its power. Have nothing to do with them" (2 Timothy 3: 1-5).

The Apostle Paul gives a list of sins that have their roots in self-love. During these times, the believer must be prepared to face an overwhelming deluge of ungodliness. The apostle prophesies that Satan will bring great destruction upon the family. Children will be disobedient to parents, and men and women will be without natural affection which refers to the lack of feelings of natural tenderness and love, as demonstrated by a mother who rejects her children or kills her baby and a father who abandons his family.

Men and women will become lovers of money and pleasure and will pursue their own selfish desires. Parenthood, sacrificial love, and care for children will no longer be considered a worthy or dignified task. If Christian parents are to save their families in the difficult times now upon us, they must shield them against the corrupt values of the society in which they live, separate them from the world's ways and customs, and refuse to let the ungodly influence their children.

Today's modern family is a far cry from the families of the 1950's. The rapid social, cultural and economic changes have transformed families and have contributed to its greater complexity and diversity. Today's version of the new trends of the modern family is exactly that – just new trends, however, "Jesus Christ is the same yesterday and today and forever" (Hebrews 13:8). Nothing changes then or now that provides a sure anchor for our faith. Sin is still sin even though rarely discussed in our new transformed family culture of today. How did this happen? There are many pathways in which they occur. For instance, Paul warns us to be on guard against all philosophies, religions, and traditions that emphasize man functioning independently from God and His written revelation. Secular humanism continues to be the biggest threat. "See to it that no one take you captive through hollow and deceptive philosophy, which depends on human tradition and the basic principles of this world rather than on Christ" (Colossians 2:8).

Some illustrations of the beliefs are: Man/universe happened by impersonal chance and evolution. Man's reason determines ethics of society making humans the ultimate authority. Moral standards are not absolute – but relative. If it makes you feel good-do it. Scripture identifies humanists this way. "They exchanged the truth of God for a lie, and worshipped and served created things rather than the Creator-who is forever praised. Amen" (Romans 1:25).

PROPHECY ABOUT THE END OF THE AGE

The world did not end on 12/21/12. There have been numerous hypothetical predictions by man in an attempt to predict the future yet they all have fallen short of the mark. However, God knows the future events to occur that will end all things as He knew the beginning. Jesus' Olivet prophecy was primarily a reply to the disciples' question,

"Tell us," they said, "when will this happen, and what will be the sign of your coming and of the end of the age?" (Matthew 24:3) Jesus gives the signs which will characterize the whole course of the last days and which will intensify as the end draws nearer. The first major sign has special importance. Jesus warns them, "Watch out that no one deceives you. For many will come in my name, claiming, 'I am the Christ,' and will deceive many" (Matthew 24:4-5).

Jesus goes on to describe the increase of wars, famines, and earthquakes which will be the beginning of sorrows and how false prophets and religious compromisers within the visible church will increase and deceive many. The false teachers will be exceedingly prevalent. There will appear within the church, ministers who are highly gifted and seemingly mightily anointed by God. Some will accomplish great things for God and preach gospel truth effectively, but they will depart from the faith and gradually turn to seducing spirits and false doctrines. Because of their former anointing and zeal for God, they will mislead many.

Therefore, professing believers will accept these new revelations even though it conflicts with the revealed Word of God. Paul refers to those who profess to be Christians and appear to be religious, yet do not manifest the power of God that can save them from sin, selfishness and immorality. Such people tolerate immorality within their churches and teach that a person may practice sin and yet inherit salvation and the kingdom of God. However, these false teachers in the church can many times be identified by their opposition or indifference to the essential truths of the gospel and instead believe the inclusiveness of all, regardless of their unrepentant sins. These distorted gospel teachings have gained a foothold in other areas where millions are involved in the occult, astrology, witchcraft, spiritism, and Satanism. The influence of demons and evil spirits will multiply greatly.

Jesus continues on in the Olivet Discourse and discusses how iniquity shall abound and the love of many shall wax cold. An unbelievable increase in immorality, shamelessness, rebellion against God, and a casting off of moral restraint will characterize the last days. Sexual perversion, fornication, adultery, pornography, drugs, ungodly music, and lustful entertainment will abound. It will be as the days of Noah when the very imaginations of human hearts were evil continually. It will be as in the days of Lot when homosexuality and all kinds of sexual perversion permeated society.

Such people may continue in shameful lust and sin while justifying their actions as common human weakness or they were born that way while persuading themselves that they are still in fellowship with the Holy Spirit and in possession of salvation. They blind themselves to the warning of Scripture, "For of this you can be sure: No immoral, impure or greedy person –such a man is an idolater-has any inheritance in the kingdom of Christ and of God. Let no one deceive you with empty words, for because of such things God's wrath comes on those who are disobedient. Therefore do not be partners with them" (Ephesians 5:5-7). A good example of how sexual sin remarks can permeate society was illustrated in a TV show of Duck Dynasty in the fall of 2013. A cultural clash occurred when the family patriarch, Phil Robertson, made comments about the sin of homosexuality in a freedom of speech manner to GQ magazine in an interview. Much heated discussions began with both sides expressing their views. The Hollywood liberals, GLAAD (Gay and Lesbian Alliance Against Defamation) and religious conservative groups were offended. Both groups either lining up with the Biblical, conservative viewpoint or the hate speech, liberal viewpoint. The Biblical viewpoint is to "love the sinner and not the sin" (a most welcome virtue). However, making it perfectly clear that sin is not to be taken lightly and should be condemned, further allowing human beings their choice for repentance. This in turn does not make Bible believer's violent bigots and citing the Bible doesn't make them bigots-it makes them bigots against sin---which is a good thing. There will always be a clash of values and warfare for the spiritual soul of the country. Therefore, any attempts by the media to deliberately misread religious America should now learn a valuable lesson from this cultural clash. God is still in control no matter what the situation.

SEVERE PERSECUTION OF GOD'S PEOPLE

Persecution in one form or another is inevitable for those who desire to live a godly life in Christ. Loyalty to Christ, to His truth, and to His righteous standards involves a constant resolve not to compromise their faith or yield to the deluge of voices calling for believers to conform to the world and to lay aside Scriptural truth. The faithful will be deprived of privilege and advantage and be ridiculed because of their godly standards. They will experience grief at seeing godliness rejected by the majority. They should all ask themselves: have we suffered persecution because of our commitment to live in a godly manner? Or is our lack of suffering a sign that we have not stood firmly for the righteousness for which Christ died?

A discussion of the inspiration and authority of Scripture is necessary in order for the reader to fully understand why Paul defends his faith during persecution. "All Scripture is God-breathed and is useful for teaching, rebuking, correcting and training in righteousness, so that the man of God may be thoroughly equipped for every good work" (2 Timothy 3:16-17). That may not seem to be a very strong reason for us to trust it but it is a good place to start. If the Bible didn't make that claim for itself, we would have to take it upon ourselves to do so. In a supernatural way, the Holy Spirit led Paul and other Bible authors to write the message of God to man. In fact Paul informs us that the spiritual truth he gave was, "not in words taught us by human wisdom but in words taught by the Spirit, expressing spiritual truths in spiritual words" (1 Corinthians 2:13). Then Paul goes on to say in verse 14 that, "the man without the Spirit does not accept the things that come from the Spirit of God, for they are foolishness to him, and he cannot understand them, because they are spiritually discerned". These verses make a tremendous claim. As mentioned under the Preface of this book, fulfilled prophecy alone is proof that the Bible is the Word of God and no other.

However, there have been throughout the history of the church those who have always refused to love sound doctrine; yet as the end draws near, the situation will grow worse. "For the time will come when men will not put up with sound doctrine. Instead, to suit their own desires, they will gather around them a great number of teachers to say what their itching ears want to hear. They will turn their ears away from the truth and turn aside to myths" (2 Timothy 4:3-4).

Many will profess to be Christians, gather at churches, appear to reverence God, but will not tolerate the original New Testament apostolic faith or the Biblical demand to separate from unrighteousness. Sound Biblical preaching from a man of God will no longer be endured or tolerated by many within the church. Those who will turn from the truth will want sermons that demand less than the true gospel. They will not accept God's Word when it speaks of repentance, sin, damnation, and the necessity of holiness and separation from the world. These professing believers will not seek pastors according to God's Word but will seek those who conform to their own self-seeking and worldly desires. They will choose preachers with gifts of charismatic and motivational skills, the ability to entertain, and a message that reassures them that they can remain a Christian while living according to the flesh.

The Holy Spirit warns all those who remain faithful to God and submit themselves to His Word to expect persecution and suffering for righteousness' sake. Furthermore, they must separate from people, churches, and institutions who deny the power of God in salvation and who preach a compromising gospel.

2

Rapture

IMMINENT RETURN OF CHRIST

The imminent return of Christ to this earth is to take His church to be with Him for eternity. The event is referred to as the *rapture*. The word itself is not in the Bible but derived from the Latin word *raptu*, which means *caught away* or *caught up*. The Latin word is equivalent to the Greek *harpazo*, translated as *caught up*. "For the Lord himself will come down from heaven, with a loud command, with the voice of the archangel and with the trumpet call of God, and the dead in Christ will rise first. After that, we who are still alive and are left will be caught up together with them in the clouds to meet the Lord in the air. And so we will be with the Lord forever" (1 Thessalonians 4:16-17).

When will the rapture take place? No one really knows when this event will occur as the exact time is not spelled out in prophecy. We are told instead to maintain an attitude and condition of readiness, for Christ said, "So you also must be ready, because the Son of Man will come at an hour when you do not expect him" (Matthew 24:44). The event could occur at any moment. That's what the word imminent means – ready to take place.

Many Pastors, Bible scholars, and Christians have differing opinions as to when the rapture will occur. Let's examine some of these views. *Pre-tribulation* – A view that the entire church (Body of Christ) will be gone before any part of the tribulation begins. What is the tribulation? Jesus speaks about special signs that will occur to indicate that the end of the age is very near. These signs will lead to and signal the return of Christ to earth after the tribulation; a specific period of terrible suffering for all the people in the world. *Mid-tribulation* – A view that Christ will rapture the church in the middle of the tribulation. *Partial-rapture theory* – Only the faithful, watchful, and praying Christians will be raptured. In other words, unfaithful Christians or professed Christians who are not really Christians at all will be left behind to suffer through the tribulation. The idea being that going through the fiery trials of the tribulation will refine them to meet the Lord at the second coming. *Pre-wrath theory*- This event occurs toward the end of the tribulation but before the great wrath of God falls.

The return of Christ to earth after the tribulation must not be confused with His unexpected descent from heaven which demonstrate that Jesus' coming refers to the rapture of believers, occurring at a time earlier than that of His final return at the end of the tribulation, known as the second coming. This would indicate the Pre-tribulation view described above and in other major passages in Scripture describing the whole seven year tribulation as written in the book of Revelation, chapters 6 through 18.

BELIEVERS RECEIVE TRANSFORMED BODIES

Paul writes that the rapture will occur in the twinkling of an eye. "Listen, I tell you a mystery: We will not all sleep, but we will all be changed-in a flash, in the twinkling of an eye, at the last trumpet. For the trumpet will sound, the dead will be raised imperishable, and we will be changed" (1 Corinthians 15:51-52). Here Paul describes the importance and essential doctrine in the Scriptures of the resurrection of the dead and then the catching up of the church believers and demonstrates how brief the moment of the rapture will be. The bodily transformation that living believers will experience at the rapture will be nearly instantaneous. One moment they will be on earth in mortal bodies, and the next moment they will meet Christ in the clouds instantly transformed into their new, glorified, resurrection bodies.

BELIEVERS DELIVERED FROM WRATH TO COME

What happens next to the raptured believers? First of all, they will be taken to His Fathers house in heaven. "In my Father's house are many rooms; if it were not so, I would have told you. I am going there to prepare a place for you. And if I go and prepare a place for you, I will come back and take you to be with me that you also may be where I am" (John 14:2-3). Christ's coming for His faithful will enable them to escape the future hour of testing that will come upon the world. "And to wait for his Son from heaven, whom he raised from the dead- Jesus, who rescues us from the coming wrath" (1 Thessalonians 1:10). Jesus had a message to the church at Philadelphia in Revelation 3:10 which was identical to Paul's promise to the Thessalonians that they would be delivered from the wrath to come at the hour of temptation. This hour includes the divinely appointed time of trial, wrath, and tribulation that will come on the entire world in the last years of this age, just prior to the establishment of Christ's kingdom on earth.

Present-day believers who hope to escape all these things that have been prophesied in the Bible will do so only by faithfulness to Christ and His Word and by constant vigilance in prayer.

JUDGMENT OF BELIEVERS (RECEIVE REWARDS)

The Christians are now in heaven and have escaped *the wrath to come*. They will now appear before the judgment seat of Christ. What exactly is that? Paul foresaw it when he wrote, "For we must all appear before the judgment seat of Christ, that each one may receive what is due him for the things done while in the body, whether good or bad" (2 Corinthians 5:10). The issue for those at the judgment seat of Christ will not be salvation. They are all God's children – forgiven and adopted on the basis of their acceptance of Christ at some point in their lives. The purpose now is to determine the degree of reward they will receive. The judgment is considered as something solemn and serious especially since it includes the possibility of damage or loss. Paul states, "If what he has built survives, he will receive his reward. If it is burned up, he will suffer loss; he himself will be saved, but only as one escaping though the flames" (1 Corinthians 3:14-15). In other words one got to heaven by the berma seat of their pants. Everything will be made manifest openly. There will be a revealing of the believer's good and bad deeds.

The bad deeds, when repented of, are forgiven in relation to eternal punishment for Paul states, "Therefore, there is now no condemnation for those who are in Christ Jesus" (Romans 8:1). However, they are still taken into account when being judged for recompense. The believer's good deeds and love are remembered by God and rewarded because God is not unrighteous to forget their work and labor of love. To sum up the good and bad deeds; the specific results of the believer's judgment will be varied. There will be either the gain or the loss of joy, divine approval, tasks and authority, position, rewards, and honor. "These have come so that your faith-of greater worth than gold, which perishes even though refined by fire- may be proved genuine and may result in praise, glory and honor when Jesus Christ is revealed " (1 Peter 1:7). In addition, any works that were done with a selfish motivation will perish in the fire just as wood, hay, and stubble are consumed. Those things that were done on earth with God's glory in mind will live on and they cannot be burned. The key elements in testing these works will be their quality and the motivation behind them.

What kind of rewards can the Christian work toward? At least five distinct crowns are mentioned in Scripture. (1) An incorruptible crown for overcoming the old sin nature. (2) A crown of rejoicing for being a soul winner. (3) A crown of life for enduring persecution and trials. (4) A crown of righteousness for eagerly looking forward to Christ's return.

(5) A crown of glory for shepherding the flock of God. The glory of the event is only beginning when all the crowns are handed out, for these rewards are not earned for personal gain. When Christians receive their crowns at the judgment seat of Christ, they will give honor to Jesus by casting them at His feet as stated in Revelation 4:10.

3

Rise of the Antichrist

THE APOSTATE CHURCH

Unlike the rapture, the coming of the antichrist will not be without warning. Several signs will point to his coming and his appearance. At least three events must occur before he makes his appearance on earth. (1) The *mystery of iniquity*, already at work in the world must intensify. (2) The *falling away* must come, (3) *he who now holds back* is taken out of the way. (Let's unpack some of the Scriptures here to grasp the meaning of these events).

The *mystery of iniquity* is a secret or a behind-the-scenes activity of evil powers throughout the course of human history, preparing the way for the apostasy and the man of sin. It is an insidious process that entraps unbelievers and prepares many within the church to turn from true faith and to accept the lie embodied in the apostate church. It involves a spirit or movement against true Biblical faith and divine law; it seeks to gain freedom from moral restraint and to take pleasure in sin. The love of many will grow cold because of a prevailing spirit of lawlessness. Matthew 24:10-12 teaches-"At that time many will turn away from the faith and will betray and hate each other, and many false prophets will appear and deceive many people. Because of the increase of wickedness, the love of most will grow cold, but he who stands firm to the end will be saved" (Matthew 24:10-12). Yet a faithful remnant will remain loyal to the apostolic faith. The apostasy, literally meaning *departure, falling away* or *abandonment* and then rebellion will occur. Multitudes within the professing church will depart from Biblical truth. This *falling away* within the church will have two dimensions. (l) Theological apostasy is the departure from and rejection of a part or all of the original teachings of Christ and the apostles. For instance in 1 Timothy 4:1 it says- "The Spirit clearly says that in later times some will abandon the faith and follow deceiving spirits and things taught by demons". Then in 2 Timothy 4:3 it further states-"For the time will come when men will not put up with sound doctrine. Instead, to suit their own desires, they will gather around them a great number of teachers to say what their itching ears want to hear". In other words, they won't listen to what the Bible says but will follow their own mis-guided ideas.

False leaders will offer salvation and cheap grace and ignore Christ's demand for repentance, separation from immorality, and loyalty to God's standards. What are the standards? 2 Peter 2:1- describes it this way-"But there were also false prophets among the people, just as there will be false teachers among you. They will secretly introduce de-structive heresies, even denying the sovereign Lord who bought them –bringing swift destruction on themselves". Therefore, many will fol-low their evil teaching that there is nothing wrong with sexual sin and because of them, Christ and his way will be scoffed at. These teachers in their greed will tell you anything to get hold of your money. But God condemned them long ago and their destruction is on the way. (2) Then there is the moral apostasy which is the severing of one's saving relationship with Christ and returning to sin and immorality. Apostates may proclaim right doctrine and New Testament teachings, yet abandon God's moral standards. Jesus gives an illustration when he says in Matthew 23:28-"In the same way, on the outside you appear to people as righteous but on the inside you are full of hypocrisy and wickedness".

Lastly, the decisive event that must occur before *the man of sin* can be revealed and the day of the Lord and its tribulation begins. This will happen after the taking out of the way of someone or something that is holding him back and then has to step out of the way. What is this someone or something? 2 Thessalonians 2:7 states- "For the secret power of lawlessness is already at work; but the one who now *holds it back* will continue to do so till he is taken out of the way". This may best be understood as referring to the Holy Spirit who alone has the power to hold back iniquity, the man of sin, and Satan. Consequently, the Holy Spirit being taken out of the way enables the man of sin to come on the scene. This does not mean He is taken out of the world, but only that His restraining influence against lawlessness and the antichrist's entrance will cease. All restraint against sin will be removed and the satanically inspired rebellion will begin. However, the Holy Spirit will still remain on earth during the tribulation to convict people of their sins, convert them to Christ, and empower them.

MAN OF SIN REVEALED

According to Bible prophecy, the next event after the rapture of the church is the rise of a false Christ to world prominence. He is called the antichrist. Paul's terms for the antichrist are the *man of sin* and the *son of perdition*. When the antichrist is revealed, the stage will be set for the terrible events of the tribulation and for the most distressing period of all history. He will be a world ruler who will make a covenant with Israel seven years before the end of the age. Here is what the Bible tells us about antichrist. He will receive power from Satan. He will receive his throne from Satan. He will receive his authority from Satan. He will be a ruler. His purpose will be conquest. He will be guilty of terrible blasphemy. He will make a peace treaty with Israel and then break it. He will put himself above everything and everyone. He will proclaim himself to be God. He will stage a miraculous resurrection. He will make war with the saints. He will have authority over the nations. His number is 666. He will kill millions of new believers. A false prophet will serve him. He will demand that his image be worshipped.

The antichrist is Satan's counterfeit. As Jesus Christ was sent by the Father, so this false Christ will be sent by Satan. Antichrist may be living today but he probably won't come forward openly as a Christ-hating world dictator until Jesus has caught up Christians from the earth at the rapture. Antichrists have been present for hundreds of years. The apostle John declared that many antichrists have already entered into the church. They are professed believers who love the world and its sinful pleasures and distort the gospel's message of the cross. However, the true identification of the antichrist will be confirmed three and one-half year later after he breaks his covenant with Israel. He becomes the world ruler, declares himself to be God, desecrates the temple in Jerusalem, forbids the worship of the Lord and devastates the land.

Additionally, the antichrist will demonstrate through the power of Satan great signs, lying wonders, and miracles in order to propagate error. Lying wonders means that they are genuine supernatural miracles that deceive people into accepting a *lie*. It is possible these demonstrations of the supernatural will be seen on television and the internet around the world. We certainly have the technical capability for this to happen. Millions of people will be impressed, deceived and persuaded by this highly persuasive and popular leader because they have no deep commitment to or love for the truth of God's word. The Apostle Paul has a stern warning to those inside or outside the church who, after adequately hearing the truth of God's word, have willingly and intentionally refused to love the truth and chose instead to take pleasure in the wickedness of the world. God will send those individuals a strong delusion so that they may never again have an opportunity to believe the truth they refused to love. They are forever doomed to believe *a lie*. This is a very stern warning that should have unbelievers shaking in their boots.

MARK OF THE BEAST-666

The account of the mark of the beast is one of the best known prophecies in all of Scripture. Even most people who have never opened a Bible are familiar with the phrase 666. The mark of the beast and its accompanying technology will be installed by the antichrist not as an end in itself, but as a means of managing the new world order that is now being created. The new world order will be a complex and complicated system to administer even for a man who can perform great lying signs and wonders.

To track the movements of people, equipment, goods, and finances will take a sophisticated system. Once these technologies are pulled together into an integrated network with common, universal standards, the antichrist will be able to fully control the buying and selling of the entire world. How will that happen? The possibilities are endless how technology might be used such as electronic identification, microchips and smart cards. Satellite and computer technology, such as GPS, can track persons, places and things. However, in order to gain total economic control of the world all people must worship the antichrist and receive a mark on their hand or forehead in order to buy or sell. Those who refuse to take the mark will be hunted down and killed. The Bible is not specific in Revelation 13 as to what the mark is —all it states is that everyone great and small, rich and poor, slave and free – has to receive a mark. Today there are a variety of ways already being used to mark ones body such as tattoos, piercing and other devices.

Bringing the world on-line has already set the stage for future events for the antichrist to control the global government, the universal monetary system and a one world religion. All of the factors together will comprise the new world order. One would have to be virtually blind not to see that we are already in these phases of execution. Not a matter of if but when- is the question. Amazing, isn't it?

We should stop here to clearly point out some of the ramifications of this system. In the last days when all of these events have evolved to make possible the global order, the system will not allow outsiders such as the body of believers to function without the mark. Anyone who serves God will be hated by the new world order of man. Therefore, it is crucial to understand that the decision to take the mark of the beast involves some form of a pledge of allegiance to the antichrist making it a spiritual decision that has only secondary economic benefits. This pledge will mean they accept the beast's system of government, finance, and religion. Eventually, it will mean that they buy into his vision, his platform, and his program.

How will this happen? The usual *LIES*. Revelation 13 specifically tells us that when the beast rises onto the world scene, his first speeches and overtures to the world community will stress his hatred for God and all those who believe in Him. As antichrist speaks blasphemies against the one true God, his supporters will join in the chorus of railings and profanities toward their Creator. It is this action, combined with their attempts to create the *kingdom of man,* in which God has no part that constitutes an eternal spiritual decision.

In this context, the Lord's solemn and eternal warning to those who would take the mark of the beast becomes completely understandable. They will seal their doom, suffer severe judgments from God and be tormented forever and ever. Antichrist may be able to kill the believers but Jesus says – "Do not be afraid of those who kill the body but cannot kill the soul. Rather, be afraid of the One who can destroy both soul and body in hell" (Matthew 10:28).

4

Great Tribulation

SEVEN YEAR TRIBULATION PERIOD BEGINS

As discussed earlier, once the antichrist is revealed the terrible events of the tribulation will occur. Two sections of the New Testament describe the events of these seven years. Matthew 24 and Revelation 6 through 16. It should be observed that many details of Christ's coming are not fully disclosed in Matthew 24. All the prophecies concerning eschatology (end times events) have not been deciphered with complete certainty but what is certain is that it will all happen according to God's perfect will and timing.

In addition, the book of Revelation is the most difficult book in the New Testament to interpret. The book communicates through dramatic apocalyptic images and symbolism depicting the consummation of the whole Bible message of redemption.

Also note that the events are ordered according to literary, rather than strictly chronological patterns. Please keep these in mind as we unfold the prophetic details indicating how mankind will suffer during these frightening times. It is the revelation of Jesus Christ which was supernaturally communicated to God's servant John while he was exiled to the island of Patmos. John was allowed to see and record certain future events so they could be an encouragement to all believers. What he saw, in most cases, was indescribable, so he used illustrations to show what it was like. When reading this symbolic language, we don't have to understand every detail – John himself didn't.

First of all we need to know the purposes of the tribulation. One purpose is to bring retribution on the world to punish sin. A second purpose is to bring Israel to the place where she can be restored to the position of spiritual favor she once held in God's eyes.

MESSAGES TO THE SEVEN CHURCHES/SEVEN SEALS

The vision John received opens with instructions for him to write to seven churches. He both commends them for their strengths and warns them about their flaws. Each letter was directed to a church then in existence but also speaks to conditions in the church throughout history, even today's churches. A stern warning to Christians who have grown apathetic and an encouragement to those who faithfully endure struggles in this world.

After the seven letters were written we are introduced to the seven seals. This is the first of three seven-part judgments. The trumpets and the bowls are the other two. Christ, as the worthy lamb who was slain, is now about to reveal another phase of God's plan for the end of human history. When each seal is broken, a portion of the books content is revealed in a vision. The seals are opened between Revelation 6.1 and 8.11.

The seventh introduces a further sequence, the seven trumpets, which are blown one by one from Revelation 8.6 to 11.15. Then at the center of the book we find visions which unveil the ultimate source of evil and its chief agents: The Dragon, the Beast from the Sea and the Beast from the Land – and also a vision of those who have somehow defeated these monsters (Chapters 12-15). This then leads into the final sequence of seven: the seven bowls of God's wrath, the final plagues which, like the plagues of Egypt, will be the means of judging the great tyrannical power and rescuing God's people from its claws.

Pouring out the seven bowls of the wrath of God begins at a point just before Christ's return to earth. A great world war will occur toward the end of these intense and severe judgments. Some of the plagues mentioned are: ugly sores, death of marine life, contaminated fresh water, unbearable heat, darkness and pain, demonic hordes, earthquakes and large hail.

To those unaccustomed to vivid descriptions of God's anger in judgment, these are disturbing images. But, unless we face the necessity of God's judgment, we will never see our desperate need for His mercy. Otherwise, we would not be inspired to repentance, obedience, or worship.

Even though suffering and death will fall on the nations during the tribulation, the majority will not repent. The Bible says, they gnawed their tongues in agony and continued to curse the God of Heaven and refused to trust Him.

However, there will be a great multitude that will turn to God during the tribulation. John refers to them as "a great multitude which no one could number, of all nations, tribes, peoples and language, standing before the throne and in front of the Lamb" (Revelation 7:9). Who is this vast crowd? The Bible describes these 144,000(the number being 12,000 from 12 tribes) bondservants of God from the sons of Israel. God will set a seal or mark upon their foreheads to indicate consecration and ownership. This seal is the exact opposite of the mark of the beast explained earlier. These two marks place the people in two distinct categories – those owned by God and those owned by Satan. These sealed believers will not fall away from God even though they may undergo intense persecution. Their eternal destiny is secure with Him.

The bowl judgments will be the last divine judgments on a wicked world before the return of Christ to reign. The bowl judgments are God's final and complete judgment on earth. The end has come! God's wrath may be hard for us to accept. In a moral universe, however, God must ultimately oppose and destroy evil. Those who join the revolt against God suffer with their leaders. Also, we must avoid the misconception that God must be fair and kind in His dealings with humanity. This view of justice is merely a projection of a human idea. People who believe this notion appeal to tolerance and forgiveness and assume God must play by our rules. In reality, God sets his own standards of justice. He uses His power according to His own moral perfection. Thus, whatever He chooses or decrees is fair, even if we don't understand or like it. Those who rebel and reject God are not rejecting a *lifestyle option*; they are rejecting truth and justice itself. Make no mistake about the fact the God is who He says He is.

5

The Millennium

BATTLE OF ARMAGEDDON

As the tribulation draws to a close, the earth will be in turmoil. Millions will have died in war or its aftermath. Satan and demons will gather together many nations under the direction of the antichrist in order to make war against God, His armies, and His people, and to destroy Jerusalem.

The center of the battle will be located in north-central Palestine called Armageddon or the mountain of Megiddo. Both sides – the antichrist and his opponents will hate the people of God. They will engage in a fierce battle and the fighting will reach Jerusalem, and the Jews living there will suffer horribly. Suddenly, when all seems hopeless, the scene will change. The second coming of Christ will occur and supernaturally intervene to destroy the antichrist and his armies and all who disobey the gospel.

SECOND COMING OF CHRIST

What is the second coming of Christ? Just as the first coming of Christ accomplished the major purpose of God to provide salvation, so the second coming of Christ will accomplish the major purpose of God to place everything in subjection to Jesus Christ as King of Kings and Lord of Lords.

In Christ's present position in heaven, He is waiting for the time when judgment will fall on His enemies, and the judgment that will take place at His second coming. There are many Old Testament passages stating that the second coming of Christ is a major event that will dramatically change the course of earthly events and bring in the promised kingdom in which Christ will reign supreme.

However, in the New Testament account, the Disciples of Christ were very slow to understand that Christ was going to leave them and then come back again. They only gradually understood that there was a time period between the first and second coming after Christ ascended. At Christ's ascension, the angels told the disciples in Acts 1:11 –

"This same Jesus, who has been taken from you into heaven, will come back in the same way you have seen Him go to heaven."

In Christ's own description of His second coming, He indicates that it will be preceded by the great tribulation. He states in Matthew 24:29-30- "Immediately after the distress of those days the sun will be darkened, and the moon will not give its light; the stars will fall from the sky, and the heavenly bodies will be shaken. At that time the sign of the Son of Man will appear in the sky, and all nations of the earth will mourn. They will see the Son of Man coming on the clouds of the sky, with power and great glory".So this will be a visible, bodily return unlike the rapture, which there is a question whether it will be visible or not. In contrast to the rapture of the church, which is a movement of the church from earth to heaven, the second coming of Christ will be a procession from heaven to earth including both saints and angels. This will be an awe inspiring event in keeping with the glory and majesty of Christ.

Jesus Christ will appear in all His glory and descend to the Mount of Olives. When His feet touch it, the mountain will split in half, forming a vast new valley stretching from the Jordan River to the Mediterranean Sea. The antichrist will be crushed in defeat. Israel will be rescued. The antichrist and his cohorts will be thrown into the lake of fire. Satan himself will be bound. Christ will prepare to ascend His throne in Jerusalem to rule in peace for 1,000 years.

What happens to those who survive the tribulation? Jesus Christ will hold two special judgments at the close of the tribulation. The first will be for the Jews who survive those terrible days. The Jews who have trusted Him will be received into His kingdom; those who rejected Him will not. A similar judgment will be held for the Gentiles (non-Jews) who live through the tribulation. Believers in Christ will be allowed to enter the millennial kingdom; unbelievers will die and await the great white throne judgment. (See Chapter 6).

THOUSAND YEAR REIGN

The battle is over and the earth is in ruins. Death and destruction lie everywhere. Satan will be bound and imprisoned for a thousand years in order that he may not deceive the nations. The imprisonment implies a complete cessation of his influence during this time.

What comes next? Rather than returning to His Father in heaven, Jesus Christ will erect His throne in Jerusalem, establish it as His capital city, reinstate the Jews as His people, and rule over the entire earth in a 1,000-year reign of peace, prosperity, and righteousness.

The Old Testament prophecies are filled with details about the new government Christ will establish when He returns. The characteristics of this reign are the following: (1) Satan will be bound. (2) Christ's reign will be shared by the faithful of His churches and perhaps also by the resurrected Old Testament saints and martyred tribulation saints. John does not mention the resurrection of the church saints who have died, for this occurred when Christ removed His church from earth and took it to heaven during the rapture. (3) The people ruled by Christ will consist of those on earth who were faithful to Christ during the tribulation and who survived until the Lord's coming as well as those born during the millennium. (4) No unsaved person will enter the kingdom. (5) Those reigning with Christ stand far above all the nations, for they will minister to and rule both Israel and the other nations. (6) There will be peace, prosperity, and righteousness throughout the earth. (7) Nature will be restored to its original order, perfection, and beauty. (8) The nations during this reign are obliged to continue in faith and obedience to Christ and His rule. However, some will choose the way of rebellion and disobedience and will be punished. (9) At the end of the thousand years, the kingdom will be delivered up by Jesus to the Father; then will begin the final and everlasting kingdom of God and the Lamb.

6

Final Judgment

FINAL REBELLION – SATAN LOOSED

As promised in Revelations, Satan will be loosed at the end of the thousand years, and a rebellion against Christ's millennial rule will immediately follow. The Bible states "when the thousand years have expired, Satan will be released from his prison and will go out to deceive the nations which are in the four corners of the earth, Gog and Magog, to gather them together to battle, whose number is as the sand of the sea. They went up on the breadth of the earth and surrounded the camp of the saints and the beloved city. Fire came down from God out of heaven and devoured them. The devil, which deceived them, was cast into the lake of fire and brimstone where the beast and the false prophets are. They will be tormented day and night forever and ever."

The thousand years of confinement will not change Satan's nature, and he will attempt to take the place of God and receive the worship and obedience that is due God alone. It had all begun sometime in eternity past, when Lucifer had looked with a jealous eye at the throne of God. In pride, he led a rebellion of angels against God and was cast out of heaven.

The question may fairly be asked why Satan will be loosed at the end of the 1,000 years of confinement. The Bible does not explain this, but it will be a demonstration of the incurable wickedness of Satan and the fact that even past the 1,000 years, his rebellion against God has not changed. It will support the concept that punishment must be eternal because wicked natures do not change. The judgment on the people who join Satan will show the extreme wickedness of human hearts, which will be pride and rebellion in spite of living in an almost perfect environment where there is full knowledge of God and full revelation of the glory of Jesus Christ. Sadly, many of those born during the millennium evidently choose to reject the visible Lordship of Christ and choose instead Satan and his lie.

Satan's rebellion is now smashed and it will be time for the final judgment. A new heaven and a new earth will soon be appearing, and the last detail of earth-business must be completed. This judgment will occur at the great white throne of God.

GREAT WHITE THRONE JUDGMENT/BOOKS/ BOOK OF LIFE OPENED

The apocalyptic prophecy concludes with the Great White Throne Judgment scene and includes the lost of all ages. We are told that the dead, small and great, will stand before the throne. Unbelievers of Old Testament days, the church age, the tribulation, and the millennium will be there as the books are opened.

At this point, according to Revelation 20:12, we find a set of books and a book being opened. What are these books? For the identity of these books we must look beyond our immediate text to other passages in God's Word. Galatians 3:10 contains the description of the book of the law. Why were the laws given in the first place? They were added after the promise was given to show men how guilty they were of breaking God's law. However, this system of law was to last only until the coming of Christ. If we could be saved by His laws, then God would not have had to give us a different way to get out of the grip of sin. The Scriptures indicate we are all its prisoners. The ONLY way out is through FAITH in Jesus Christ; the way of escape is open to all who believe in Him.

Additionally, salvation in Christ does not mean that the law has no value. Rather, justification by faith establishes the law according to the right purpose and function. Through the regenerating work of the Holy Spirit, the believer becomes capable of honoring and obeying God's moral law. Regenerating meaning a re-creating and transformation of the person.

Revelation 20:12 indicates that some of the books at this Great White Throne Judgment will be books of a person's works, for "the dead were judged according to what they had done as recorded in the books." The same thing is said in verse 13… "They were judged every man according to their works." In connection with this thought, it is well to consider Ecclesiastes 12:14: "For God will bring every deed into judgment, including every hidden thing, whether it is good or evil." In this final hour the books of one's works or deeds will be opened.

Not only will the dead be judged out of the books according to their works, but two other books will be opened. One is called the *Book of Life*; the other the *Lamb's Book of Life* which is Jesus' Book of Life. (Jesus is often referred to as a Lamb). These are definitely not the same. There are two major differences between these two books of life.

The term *Book of Life* relates to the custom of keeping records of one's family tree. In God's dealing with Moses concerning the sin of the people of Israel, Moses said in Exodus 32:32 –"But now, please forgive their sin – but if not, then blot me out of the book you have written." Then in verse 33, the Lord said to Moses-"Whosoever has sinned against me I will blot out of my book." In the New Testament, the *Book of Life* refers to the register of those who have received eternal life. For instance, Jesus says in Revelation 3:5-"He who overcomes will, like them, be dressed in white. I will never blot out his name from the *Book of Life*, but will acknowledge his name before my Father and his angels. What about the names in the *Book of Life*? Who is in, who is out? According to this Biblical passage, any person who experiences the new birth, but later refuses to preserver in faith and to conquer, will have his name taken out of the *Book of Life*. However, the conqueror, who has experienced the new birth and remains constant in his victory over sin, the world, and Satan will *not* have his name removed from the *Book of Life* but will be honored by Christ before His Father and the angels. **BEWARE!** Get your name in the *Book of Life* and keep it there at all costs since Scripture further states that whosoever was not found written in the *Book of Life* was cast into the lake of fire. It bears repeating these warnings of everlasting destruction.

Though the doctrine of eternal punishment is repugnant to the unsaved world and troubles even those who are saved, a thorough appreciation of the destiny of the wicked will do much to further zeal for preaching the Gospel and for winning souls for Christ. The idea of flames and anguish appalls us. However, these are the people who intentionally and willfully chose not to trust in Christ. They turned their backs on God's grace deciding to leave Him out of their lives. It was their own choice.

God is not vengeful and antagonistic. He does not cause suffering just for the sport of it. His judgment stems from His holiness, and He is absolutely righteous and holy. No one will receive one bit more or less than he deserves because God can only judge rightly.

7

The New Heavens and New Earth

NEW WORLD CREATED

The character and significance of the new heaven and the new earth and the New Jerusalem occupy the remaining two chapters of the book of Revelation. John recorded in his vision of the new heaven and the new earth stating – "Then I saw a new heaven and a new earth, for the first heaven and the first earth had passed away, and there was no longer any sea" (Revelation 21: l). As brought out earlier, the inference is that a new heaven and a new earth are entirely new creations and not similar to the old creation. The summary of Peters' statements in 2 Peter 3:10-12, are that the Lord is surely coming as unexpectedly as a thief in the night. The heavens will pass away with a terrible noise and the heavenly bodies will disappear in fire, and the earth and everything on it will be burned up. Peter goes on to say that since everything around us is going to melt away, what holy, godly lives we should be living—he is giving us an advanced warning.

Why would a loving God do such a terrible thing? Since sin has contaminated the earth and universe, God has determined to completely destroy them by fire as He did in Sodom and Gomorrah. God will not allow sin to go unpunished forever.

How might the elements be destroyed by fire and the earth and everything in it laid bare? To unpack some of Paul's declarations in Colossians 1:16 when he affirms the creative activity of Christ. All things, both material and spiritual, owe their existence to the work of Christ as the active agent in creation. All things hold together and are sustained by Him. Therefore, it wouldn't take much of a stretch of the imagination that He could undo all things created. Having stated all of this —it is possible that the destruction of the physical earth and heaven could be a gigantic explosion in which all goes back to nothing. A nuclear episode looms over humanity on a daily basis as we struggle with countries that have the capability of unleashing nuclear weapons. Syria, North Korea, Iran, the United States and others all have the capability of bringing about these changes.

Out of this, God could create a new heaven and a new earth as a base for eternity.

In any case, the new earth will be totally different from the old earth, and one of these differences is that there will no longer be any seas. All the landmarks will be gone, and the new earth will look different.

THE NEW JERUSALEM

John in his vision was immediately directed to the New Jerusalem, which is the primary object of the revelation rather than the new heaven and new earth. He wrote, "I saw the Holy City, the New Jerusalem, coming down out of heaven from God, prepared as a bride beautifully dressed for her husband" (Revelation 21:2).

The fact that the New Jerusalem is not said to be created at this time but, rather, comes down out of heaven from God implies that it was in existence in the previous period – that is, in the millennial kingdom. As millennial passages make clear, there will be no gigantic city such as the New Jerusalem on earth in the millennial period. If it is in existence at that time, it must be a satellite located in space like Star Wars, though the Bible does not comment on this entirely.

What are some of the outstanding features of the New Jerusalem?

The condensed version of what John saw in Revelation 21 and 22 is as follows: It started out as previously mentioned –as beautiful as a bride dressed for her husband. Several more descriptions follow such as: where God dwells with men; immense in size; a jeweled foundation; a 216 foot high wall of jasper; 12 gates of pearl, always open; buildings and streets of gold; illuminated by God's glory; a crystal river; trees of life for healing (fruit to keep us healthy); the throne of God. There will also be some things missing from our heavenly home: no sea; no more curse; no tears; no death; no pain; no sorrow; no night; no temple; no sun; no moon; no impurity; no deceit. What a wonderful place and everyone will live happily ever after.

Though the wonder of heaven and the eternal state is difficult to understand in our present limitation, it is absolutely certain that this is our destiny and this is what we have a right to expect as those who are saved by the grace of God. Furthermore, it is not something that is distantly removed. Christ is coming soon, and when He comes, blessings will fall on those who have believed and received the prophecies of the Bible. Some have been confused about the literal meaning of the expression –"Behold, I am coming soon" (Revelation 22:7). The verse was uttered almost two thousand years ago. It is more accurately translated, "Behold, I come suddenly." This saying does not refer to an appointed time soon to come but means that His coming will take place suddenly and without warning.

8

Middle East Tension

GOD'S COVENANT WITH ISRAEL

God's relationship with His people is described throughout the Bible in terms of *covenant*. By understanding God's covenant with the patriarchs (Abraham, Issac, and Jacob), we learn about how God wants us to live in our covenant relationship with Him. The ultimate goal of God's covenant with humankind is to bring salvation, not just to one nation (Israel) but to the whole human race. This covenant was fulfilled through the coming of the Lord Jesus Christ as redeemer, when Christians began to spread the message of the gospel throughout the world. The call to covenant remembrance and renewal is relevant today. The New Testament is God's covenant with us as we read and study His revelation to us with its promises and stipulations as proclaimed in the preaching of God's Word. Note that God's promise of an *eternal covenant* with His people was always conditional upon their obedience to His revealed will.

Where does Israel stand today with God's covenant? Israel stands squarely in the crosshairs of evil and determined enemies who want nothing more than to finish the job Hitler started more than seven decades ago. Today, Israel is living in the most difficult and dangerous days in modern history, a prophecy which is being fulfilled before our eyes.

Israel continues to repeat its history in areas of conflict with Palestinians, Hamas and Isis. Al Qaeda and Isis both have fighters in Gaza and their ultimate goal is to establish an Islamic caliphate. Right now the enemies surrounding this tiny nation have the ability to launch thousands of rockets and missiles into Israel's cities. How can we ignore the fact that Iran has missiles that are capable of striking anywhere in Israel, as well as in Europe, the United Kingdom and the United States? The devastation would be catastrophic and the loss of innocent life would be immense. Thousands would die – Arabs and Jews alike.

Truces continue to be broken, violence and death continues as rockets are exchanged and peace is deemed impossible. Most of the world is turning a blind eye to the threat of Iran and its evil mullahs. Even worse, placing our nation on the side of those who wish to destroy Israel will bring down God's judgment on our land. Genesis 12:3 clearly tells us that God will bless those who bless Israel and curse those who curse Israel. Throughout history every empire and nation that has raised up its hand against the Jewish people have been harshly judged. The United States will be no exception.

World leaders, including the Obama administration, are pushing Israel to divide the Holy City in the name of false promises of peace. The pretense that the Palestinians have a functioning government is a necessary fiction to those who insist on a peace process.

Jeremiah (Old Testament Prophet) warned the people in Judah and Jerusalem that declaring peace, peace when there is no peace was a forewarning for what was to come. He called them to repentance to renew their covenant with God. The plea was rebuffed in scorn and judgment fell on Jerusalem and the temple. God has declared by His eternal promise that Jerusalem is His and cannot be taken from His Chosen People.

The desire for peace in the Middle East is ongoing yet the plans for implementation pose a great danger to Israel. With the outcome of the elections in November 2014, it may place America back on the side of

God's Chosen People if some changes are made to remain an ally of Israel rather than an enemy. The battle belongs to the Lord as we see that the news is in reality a spiritual battle against the powers of evil and that God remains in control of all events. Amen.

ISLAM ON THE RISE

As this book is being written, America finds itself bogged down in an unprovoked, worldwide war with radical Islamic terrorists with no end in sight. What do we need to know about Islam? That would be another writing of another book. The condensed readers digest version is as follows.

It is nearly impossible to pick up any national newspaper today, go on-line, or watch any national news broadcast without hearing about the escalating, radical Islamic terrorist attacks around the world. Consider the attacks in Paris, France in January 2015, the beheadings of American journalists and Japanese hostages and other unprovoked atrocities on the innocent in Boko Haram. Because of the attacks by Islamic terrorists, there is today a parade of nations who have entered the war with Islam. Tragically, many Americans and Christians do not understand the danger radical Islam poses for America and Israel. How many more 9/11 attacks do we need to wake us up? Why does using the term "Islamic Radicals-ISIS" become a "see no evil, hear no evil, do no evil" philosophy?

America is stumbling in the fog of political correctness while lacking the intellectual honesty to admit that radical Islam has every intention of conquering Western civilization. After all, we in our multiculturalism want to respect and tolerate everyone—which in itself is a wonderful quality to have. However, history supports that the many terrorist attacks in which America did not and still does not fully respond is seen by radical Islams as Americans weak and powerless to stop their terrorist attacks. We as a people, must recognize that just because we cannot see the enemy, does not mean the enemy is not there. They are not coming, they are here and we are on their radar.

For instance, there is a growing threat of Islamic extremists all across American campuses. Anti-Semitic behavior is evolving with student uprising, swastika paintings and chanting Allah Akabar. Muhammad taught a doctrine of triumphalism, meaning that it is God's (Allah's) will for the law of Islam to rule the world. What we underestimate is the hatred and teachings in the Quran against Christian and Jews. The declaration of war has become a clear and present danger.

Today, the religious beliefs on Islam and Israel remain in total opposition to each other. For Islam, the land of Israel is a Holy possession consecrated for future Muslim generations until Judgment Day. This is a religious war that Islam cannot and must not win. However, we know the end of His-Story as outlined in this book. It was God Himself who gave the land to Abraham, Isaac and Jacob and their descendants forever. It bears repeating that God holds the future of Israel in His hands and it will be a glorious eternal future. To God Be The Glory! God's name is not Allah!

THE BLESSED HOPE

Is there any hope? Each one of us is presently on a journey to another country, more real than anything we have experienced here on earth, for everything here on earth will one day be destroyed, but the better country will have no end. It will not decay, it will not diminish, and neither shall its inhabitants. Our lives did not begin the moment we were conceived in the eternal mind of God in eternity past. Our lives will not end the moment we die on this earth; in fact, in view of eternity, they will have scarcely begun.

Today we live in the shadow of death, fearing it, fearing the end, our end. Nothing could be further from the truth. For the Christian, death has lost its sting. Long after this world has passed into faded memory we will be more fully alive than we have ever been, living the immortal life God always intended us to live. A trillion years will pass, and it will be less than a moment in eternity for it is but a grain of sand on an endless beach of eternity.

This may be the most important reflection of our entire life. It is not enough to know that heaven exists or that the better country will be greater than our greatest hopes.

A simple prayer, sincere and heartfelt, with as much faith as we can muster at the moment is sufficient. Such as, "Lord, I've finally understood how much you love me and all you have done to cancel out and forgive my sins through your death on the cross. I believe this to be true through faith. I ask that you would forgive me, a sinner, and grant me entrance into the better country by your grace and mercy. I realize I don't deserve it; I am trusting entirely in your grace. I pray this in Jesus name. Amen."

With this description of heaven on earth complete, the Bible comes to an end as does HIS-STORY. When we think of the wonders of that home awaiting us, where the Lord Himself will dwell with us, we can only say with John in Revelation 22:20-**"Even so, come, Lord Jesus"**.

CPSIA information can be obtained
at www.ICGtesting.com
Printed in the USA
FSOW01n1618020117
29121FS